I
Vegetaria

Irish
Vegetarian Cookery
Traditional & Modern

2nd Edition

*editor:*Patrick Cotter

Killeen

For
Mom, Dad
and in memory of
Colin Long 1969-1993

Published by
Killeen Books,
Killeen,
Blackrock Village,
Cork City,
Ireland.

Distributed in Britain
by Central Books Ltd.
London.

First published by Three Spires 1993
This revised edition is published by Killeen Books in 1996

ISBN 1-873548-34-6

Set in Adobe Garamond and Koch Roman by the publishers.
Colour separations prepared by Upper Case Ltd.

Printed by the Guernsey Press on Munken Offset Woodfree
which is also chlorine and acid free. Chlorine-free means that
the paper is made without using the most damaging pollut-
ant associated with paper production. Acid-free means the
paper will not slowly self-combust, turning yellow and
brittle with age.

Preface

Welcome to the second edition of *Irish Vegetarian Cookery* combining the best of traditional meat-free recipes with innovative restaurant cuisine. The Irish have a reputation for being heavy meat-eaters but prior to this century meat was a rare thing on most people's plates. Dairy products, bread and fresh vegetables formed the core of the peasant's diet. The population of the country exploded in the last century with the aid of the potato, a highly nutritious food loaded with vital vitamins and fibre. The collapse of Ireland's population along with the potato crops only emphasises how important a lacto-vegetarian diet was to most Irish people. Milk and butter mixed with potatoes formed a diet which produced peasants healthier and more robust than the town-dwelling working-class who tended to survive on milk, butter and bread.

Thankfully the days when a vegetarian diet was a poverty-choice rather than a life-choice have passed for most people. Irish vegetarians are no longer restricted to potatoes, bread and milk: as this book amply illustrates, Ireland is in the middle of a culinary revolution. From the Aran Islands to Dublin, Cavan to Cork, Irish chefs are producing dishes of genius with whatever ingredients they can lay their hands on. So wether you are a vegan or a lacto-vegetarian or even an occasional carnivore like myself who loves good food there'll be plenty of things to interest you here. Try the recipes yourself at home but don't miss the chance to visit some of the brilliant restaurants in this book and taste the latest creations of Irish vegetarian cuisine — It's not just a load of potatoes!

For those who might be interested the Irish Vegetarian Society can be contacted at P.O. Box 3010, Dublin 4. Keep an eye out in the bookshops for two excellent guides: *The Bridgestone Vegetarian's Guide to Ireland* by John and Sally McKenna and *The Vegetarian and Vegan Guide to Ireland* (updated annually) from the East-Clare Co-Op Tel: 061-921641

Contents

Restaurant Recipes

Nettle Soup

Ingredients

25g (1 oz) butter, 50g (2 oz) oatmeal, 600ml
(1 pint) of washed, finely-chopped, young,
spring-time, stinging-nettle tops, 1 large
chopped onion, 600ml (1 pint) milk, 300ml
(½ pint) vegetable stock,
salt and pepper, chopped fresh parsley,
300ml (½ pint) cream

Method

Melt the butter and fry the oatmeal until brown.
Pour in the stock and milk. Bring to the boil.
Add the nettles and onion, salt and pepper.
Simmer for 45 minutes. Add parsley and cream.
Liquidise if desired. Reheat before serving.

※

Cream Of Mushroom Soup

Ingredients

40g (1½ oz) butter, 1 large onion finely chopped, 2 stalks of celery finely chopped, 350g (12 oz) of finely chopped mushrooms, 25g (1 oz) plain flour, 25g (1 oz) butter, 600ml (1 pint) vegetable stock, 150ml (5 fl oz) cream, 1 teaspoon of dried mixed herbs, paprika, salt and pepper, 4 button mushrooms sliced lengthways and fried until brown

Method

Melt the butter in a saucepan. Fry onion and celery until soft. Add finely chopped mushrooms, herbs, salt and pepper. Cook gently until mushroom juice evaporates. Stir in flour and cook for 1-2 minutes. Add stock and bring to the boil, stirring occasionally. Add cream, whisk and reheat without boiling. Garnish each bowl with pre-fried mushroom slices and sprinkles of paprika.

Pea Soup

Ingredients

25g (1 oz) butter, 1 onion chopped, 1 carrot diced, 1 clove garlic crushed, 2 celery sticks chopped, 225g (8 oz) dried marrow fat peas soaked overnight, 750ml water, 750ml vegetable stock, 1 teaspoon
dried mixed herbs, salt and pepper,
90ml (4 tablespoons) cream

Method

Melt butter in saucepan. Add the onion and carrot and cook gently until onion is softened. Add the garlic and celery and cook for 5 minutes. Drain the peas and add to the saucepan along with the water, stock, herbs and salt and pepper to taste. Cover and boil for ten minutes, then simmer for 2 to 3 hours, until the peas are soft. Allow to cool slightly, then liquidise with cream to a smooth paste. Add more cream or water if too thick. Reheat the soup before serving. Garnish with mint.

Potato Soup

Ingredients

1kg (2 lb) potatoes peeled and diced, 2 leeks
peeled and chopped or 2 onions if preferred,
25g (1 oz) butter, 450ml (¾ pint) milk,
450ml (¾ pint) vegetable stock,
salt and pepper, 1 clove of garlic peeled and
crushed (optional), 90ml
(4 tablespoons) cream

Method

Melt the butter in a saucepan. Add the garlic and
vegetables and cook gently until soft. Pour in the
milk and stock. Add salt and pepper to taste.
Bring to the boil and simmer gently for 1 hour.
Whisk in cream and reheat before serving.

Brotchen Roy

Ingredients

3 leeks, 25g (1 oz) butter, 75g (3 oz) flake
oatmeal, 600ml (1 pint) vegetable stock,
300ml (½ pint) milk, salt and pepper to taste,
a pinch of mace, chopped parsley,
2 tablespoons of cream

Method

Wash the leeks thoroughly and chop into chunks.
Melt the butter gently in a saucepan not allowing it to brown. Add the oatmeal and fry it in the
butter, stirring until golden brown. Still stirring,
pour on the stock and milk. Add the chopped
leeks, salt, pepper and mace. Bring to the boil,
and then simmer for about 30 minutes until the
broth is thick. Put the soup through a sieve or
liquidise in a blender. Reheat gently. Stir in the
cream and parsley not allowing the soup to boil
again before serving with Irish soda bread.

Champ

Ingredients

450g (1 lb) potatoes, 8 spring onions or 1
onion, 90ml milk, 50g (2 oz) butter,
salt and pepper

Method

Peel and slice the potatoes and simmer in a
saucepan of salted water until tender. Drain and
mash well and keep hot. Chop the spring onions
using the green as well as the white parts or peel
and chop the onion. Cook the chopped onions
in the milk until soft. Beat the hot milk, onions
and pepper into the potatoes. The mixture
should be soft and fluffy but not sloppy. Pile
into a warm serving dish. Make a hole in the
centre and put in the butter. For an interesting
variation cook two crushed cloves of garlic with
the onions in step 3.

Colcannon

Ingredients

450g (1 lb) potatoes, salt and pepper,
450g (1 lb) white cabbage, 100ml milk,
100ml cream, 1 onion,
100g (4 oz) butter, chopped parsley.

Method

Peel, boil and mash the potatoes. Allow to cool a little, then add cream. Cook the cabbage in boiling salted water until tender. Drain well, and chop. Peel and chop the onion finely. Add the onions to the milk. Bring to the boil and simmer until tender. Add the cooked cabbage, onions and milk to the potatoes. Season with pepper, and more salt if required. Keep stirring over the heat, without letting the Colcannon brown. Mix in the butter until melted.

Beetroot and Potato

Ingredients

75g (3 oz) butter, 3 medium-sized cooked
beets, peeled and sliced. 2 Small onions
sliced, 50g (2 oz) flour, 300ml (½ pint) milk
mixed with 50ml cream, salt and pepper, 1
teaspoon sugar, 1 tablespoon vinegar, 700g
(1½ lb) mashed potato, kept hot.

Method

Heat a little of the butter and fry onions in it
until soft, but do not let them brown. Heat the
rest of the butter, stir in the flour and cook for
about 1 minute. Then add the milk and cream
stirring all the time. Season well with salt and
pepper. Stir in the sugar and the vinegar and
cook for about 1 minute, then add the beet
slices. Make a circle of the hot mashed potatoes,
place the beetroot and sauce in the middle.

Creamed Cabbage

Ingredients

1kg (2¼ lb) white cabbage, 50g (2 oz) butter,
25g (1 oz) flour, pinch of grated nutmeg,
300ml milk, 300ml cream, salt and pepper

Method

Trim the cabbage, removing the stalk, cut into eighths and blanch for 5 minutes in boiling salted water. Drain well, then cut into strips. Heat the butter, stir in the flour and cook for 1 minute, then gradually add the milk and cream, then the nutmeg, stirring well to avoid lumps. Add the cabbage and bring back to the boil. Cover and cook gently for 15 minutes, stirring from time to time. Serve the cabbage, while still crunchy.

Baked Onions

Ingredients

4 large onions, unpeeled, salt and pepper,
some butter

Method

Place the onions in an oven proof dish. Pour in
enough water to the depth of one third of the
onions height. Bake in a moderate oven for
about 1½ hours, or until the onions are soft.
Sprinkle with salt and pepper. Just before serving top each onion with a knob of butter.
Oven: 160°C

Creamed Swedes

Ingredients

450g (1 lb) swedes, salt and pepper,
25g (1 oz) butter, 2 tablespoons cream,
a pinch of paprika

Method

Peel and cut up the swedes. Put in a saucepan of
cold, salted water. Bring to the boil and simmer
until tender. Drain and mash. Mix in the butter.
Season well with pepper. Add the paprika and
stir in the cream. Serve hot.

Fried Parsnips

Ingredients

4 parsnips, 100g (4 oz) butter, salt and pepper

Method

Wash and clean the parsnips, cut across in short pieces, about 2.5cm (1 inch). Add seasoning to water and boil for about half an hour. Drain and dry. Heat the butter in a pan and fry parsnips in it. Brown under grill.

Parsnip Cakes

Ingredients

450g (1 lb) parsnips, 75g (3 oz) flour, pinch garam masala, 50g (2 oz) melted butter, salt and pepper, 1 large egg beaten, 4 slices of stale bread reduced to crumbs, butter for frying

Method

Peel and slice the parsnips, then boil in salted water until tender. Drain and mash them well. Add the flour, garam masala, melted butter, salt and pepper and form into flat cakes. Dip into the beaten egg, then into breadcrumbs and fry in hot butter until brown on both sides.

Boxty Cakes

Ingredients

675g (1½ lb) cooked mashed potatoes, 675g
(1½ lb) raw potatoes, peeled and grated, some
milk, a pinch of salt, 675g (1½ lb) flour,
butter for serving.

Method

Mix the raw and cooked potatoes together, and
season to taste with a pinch of salt. Work in
enough flour and milk to give a pliable dough.
Knead well and roll out. Shape into 4 rounds.
Place on a greased tray and bake in a preheated
oven for 30-45 minutes at 160°C. Butter and
serve hot.

Spicy Boxty Cakes

Ingredients

225g (9 oz) cooked, mashed potatoes, 225g (9 oz) cooked mashed carrots, 450g (1 lb) raw potatoes peeled and grated, 450g (1 lb) flour, 150g (6 oz) precooked mushy peas, some milk, ½ teaspoon turmeric, 2 teaspoons of garam masala, a pinch of salt.

Method

Mix together the cooked and raw vegetables. Sieve the flour, salt and spices into vegetable mixture. Mix to form dough, adding milk if necessary. Repeat steps 4-8 as for ordinary boxties.

Potato And Thyme Cakes

Ingredients

450g (1 lb) potatoes, 25g (1 oz) butter, 100g
(4 oz) plain flour, 2 tablespoons of fresh
thyme or 2 teaspoons of dried thyme,
75g (3 oz) butter for frying, salt

Method

Scrub potatoes and boil for 20-30 minutes.
Drain and allow to cool for a moment. Peel and
mash. Add butter, salt and thyme. Mix with
flour and form a dough. On a floured surface,
roll out dough to a thickness of 1 cm and cut
into 5 cm squares. Heat butter for frying in pan
and fry cakes until crispy and golden on both
sides.

Lyonaise Potatoes

Ingredients

450g (1 lb) potatoes, 2 large onions thinly
sliced, 250ml cream, 3 cloves of garlic
crushed, salt and pepper, parsley

Method

Peel and wash potatoes and cut into slices. Place
the potatoes and onion in alternate layers into
an oven proof dish, sprinkling each layer with
salt and pepper. Sprinkle top layer with parsley
and garlic. Pour over the cream. Place in a preheated oven at 200°C and leave for 45-60 minutes or until tender.

Potato and Onion Mash

Ingredients

1kg (2 lb) potatoes, 1 large onion finely chopped, 2 tablespoons of butter, 1 teaspoon honey, a drop of milk, 1 teaspoon of thyme, salt and pepper

Method

Peel and wash potatoes. Boil for 25-30 minutes. Melt a tablespoon of butter in a pan and fry onions, add honey and continue frying until onions are golden brown. Drain potatoes and mash, add butter and milk. Season with salt, pepper and thyme. Mix in onions.

Potato and Carrot Omelette

Ingredients

675g (1½ lb) potatoes, 2 carrots diced, 2 onions chopped, 2 cloves garlic crushed, 6 eggs, salt and pepper, mixed herbs, 4 oz butter for frying

Method

Wash potatoes and boil for 25-30 minutes. Drain and allow to cool. Heat butter and fry carrots for three minutes. Add onion and garlic and fry for a further three minutes until golden, then set aside. Beat eggs in a large basin. Peel and slice potatoes. Mix everything in with the eggs. Reheat frying pan, add mixture and cook until the egg congeals. Slip the pan under a preheated grill and leave until topside of omelette is golden.

Potato And Mushroom Pie

Ingredients

1kg (2 lb) potatoes, 500g (1 lb) mushrooms, sliced in half, 75g (3 oz) butter, 300ml cream, 4 egg yolks, 1 onion chopped, salt and pepper, 2 tablespoons parmesan cheese

Method

Wash and peel potatoes, cut into cubes and cook for 25-30 minutes. Drain and mash. Melt 25g (1oz) butter and fry onion and mushrooms for about 5 minutes. Add seasoning and remove from heat. Stir in 50ml of cream. Mix potatoes with egg yolks, remaining butter and cream, season with salt and pepper. Preheat oven to 200°C. Spoon half of potato mixture into an oven proof pie dish and top with mushroom mixture, cover with remaining potatoes, cover with grated cheese and bake for 20 minutes.

Vegetarian Shepherd's Pie

Ingredients

225g (8 oz) yellow or green split peas, 50g (2 oz) butter, 3 large onions diced, 1 clove garlic crushed, 1 teaspoon dried mixed herbs, 1 can of tomatoes, 2 tablespoons of soya sauce, 1 teaspoon thyme,   700g (1½ lb) potatoes cooked and mashed, 2 large carrots cooked and sliced.

Method

Put the peas into a saucepan of water and boil gently for 45 minutes. Preheat the oven to 200°C. Gently fry two of the onions in the butter in a large saucepan for 10 minutes. Add the garlic, mixed herbs, tomatoes, soya sauce, peas, carrots and salt and pepper to taste. Put aside. Mix the remaining onion and thyme with the potatoes and season with salt and pepper. Spoon the pea mixture into a greased, shallow, oven-dish. Spread the potatoes over the top, flatten with a wooden spoon, then with a fork draw ridges across the surface. Bake the pie for 45 minutes or until the potatoes are golden.

Potato and Tomato Bake

Ingredients

4 garlic cloves peeled, 1 teaspoon dried mixed herbs, 300ml (½ pint) water, 8 potatoes thickly sliced, 4 large tomatoes skinned, seeded and sliced, salt and pepper.

Method

Put the garlic, mixed herbs and water in a pan and simmer for 20-30 minutes. Leave to cool. Crush the garlic with a pestle or the back of a fork until it forms a smooth mixture with the water and herbs. Spoon half the mixture into a small oven-dish. Layer the potatoes and tomatoes alternately on top and season well with salt and pepper. Spoon over the remaining garlic mixture. Cover and cook in a preheated, moderate oven 180°C for 1 hour or until the potatoes are tender.

Buttermilk Stew

Ingredients

2 tablespoons oil, 2 carrots diced finely, 1 potato diced finely, 1 onion finely chopped, 225g (8 oz) button mushrooms sliced, 1 red pepper diced, 1 green pepper diced, 2 cloves garlic crushed, 1 tin (size to taste) sweet corn drained, 600ml (1 pint) buttermilk, 200ml cream, 1 vegetable stock cube, 1 teaspoon dried mixed herbs, a dash of soya sauce.

Method

Gently fry the carrots, potato and onion for three minutes without browning. Add garlic, peppers and stock cube. Cook for 1 minute. Pour in buttermilk with mixed herbs. Bring to boil. Allow to simmer for 20 minutes. Add cream, sweet corn, soya sauce and salt and pepper. Return to boil before serving with pasta shells or swirls.

Buttermilk

Ingredients

15g (½ oz) sugar, 15g (½ oz) yeast, 300ml (½ pint) warmed water, 300ml (½ pint) milk

Method

Cream the sugar with the yeast. Pour the milk into the warmed water. Gradually stir in the sugar and yeast. Cover and leave at room temperature for a day. The liquid should smell slightly sour and taste slightly sour. Strain and the buttermilk is ready to use, or refrigerate.

Brown Scones

Ingredients

225g (8 oz) plain flour, 225g (8 oz)
wholemeal flour, a pinch of salt, 2 teaspoons
baking powder, 50g (2 oz) sugar,
100g (4 oz) butter,
1 egg beaten, 1 cup of milk.

Method

Mix plain flour and whole wheat flour. Add salt,
baking powder and sugar. Rub in the butter
with your fingers. Add beaten egg to milk, and
gradually mix in enough milk to make a soft
dough. Knead lightly and turn onto a floured
surface. Cut into rounds 2.5 cm thick and place
on a greased baking tray and bake at 220°C for
20 minutes approx.

Barmbrack

Ingredients

300ml (½ pint) of black tea, 350g (12 oz) brown sugar, 225g (8 oz) raisins, 225g (8 oz) sultanas, 50g (2 oz) butter or margarine, 1 large egg beaten, 50g (2 oz) cherries chopped, 50g (2 oz) candied peel, 25g (1 oz) almonds chopped, 275g (10 oz) flour, 1 heaped teaspoon baking powder

Method

Dissolve the sugar in the tea. Add the raisins and sultanas and leave to soak overnight. Melt the butter and mix in with the beaten egg, cherries, candied peel and almonds. Sieve the flour and baking powder and add to the egg and fruit mixture, mixing thoroughly. Grease a 20cm (8 inch) cake tin and turn in the mixture. A ring or coin, wrapped in grease-proof paper, can be added to mixture at this stage. Bake in a moderate oven 180°C for 1½ hours.

Soda Bread

Ingredients

450g (1 lb) flour, 1 teaspoon bicarbonate of soda, 1 tablespoon salt, 300ml (½ pint) buttermilk or soured milk, 1 egg beaten

Method

Sieve the dry ingredients together in a large mixing bowl. Make a well in the centre and add the buttermilk and egg. Knead until a smooth, soft dough forms. Shape the dough into a flat cake and place on a greased sheet. Cut a deep cross into the dough so the bread can rise without splitting its crust. Bake in a hot oven for about 35 minutes or until browned and risen. Remove from the oven. If the bread is cooked it will sound hollow when tapped on the bottom. Oven: 220°C

Brown Wholemeal Bread

Ingredients

350g (12 oz) wholemeal flour, 350g (12 oz)
plain flour, 1 teaspoon salt, 2 teaspoons baking powder, 2 tablespoons bran, 600ml
(1 pint) buttermilk

Method

Mix all the dry ingredients in a large bowl. Stir
in the buttermilk. Grease a 20cm (8 inch) cake
tin, spoon in the mixture and cover with tinfoil.
Bake in an oven for 1 hour.
Oven: 220°C

Porter Cake

Ingredients

450g (1 lb) flour, 1 teaspoon of baking powder, a pinch of salt, 1 teaspoon of mixed spice
225g (8 oz) butter, 225g (8 oz) brown sugar,
1 teaspoon nutmeg, 450g (1 lb) mixed dried
fruit, grated rind of 1 lemon, 3 eggs beaten,
300ml stout (try Beamish, the only Irish stout
on the market sure to be brewed in Ireland)

Method

Sieve the flour with the salt into a mixing bowl.
Mix the baking powder, sugar and spice. Rub in
the butter. Add the dried fruit, mixing thoroughly. Mix the stout with the beaten eggs and
blend into the cake mixture. Grease and line a
20cm (8 inch) cake tin. Pour in the mixture and
bake in a moderately hot oven 160° for an hour,
then lower heat to 150° and bake for a further 2
hours. Allow to cool in the tin. This cake's
flavour improves if left wrapped in foil for at
least a week before eating.

Kinsale Bread

Ingredients

15g (½ oz) yeast, 400ml warm water,
2 tablespoons sugar, 600g (1½ lb) whole
wheat flour, ½ teaspoon salt,
50ml molasses, 100ml honey

Method

Preheat oven to 225°C. Dissolve yeast in 100ml warm water and one tablespoon sugar. Set aside. Take half of the flour and make a batter with the yeast mixture and remaining warm water. Cover the bowl with a damp cloth and let stand for 15 minutes. Add the rest of the flour, salt, molasses, sugar and honey. Beat with a wooden spoon until batter is stiff. Knead on a floured surface for 10 minutes. Place dough in pan, cover and place in a warm place for 1 hour or until dough doubles in size. Bake for 45 minutes, turning the pan in the opposite direction halfway through the cooking time. Remove from oven and place on a wire rack. Let bread stand for 20 minutes, remove from tin and cool thoroughly.

Potato and Apple Pie

Ingredients

450g (1 lb) mashed potatoes, 50g (2 oz)
butter, 100g (4 oz) flour, a pinch of salt
½ teaspoon baking powder, 3-4 apples,
2 tablespoons sugar, 25g (1 oz) butter,
½ teaspoon cinnamon

Method

Mix the butter into the freshly mashed potatoes.
Sift the flour with the salt, cinnamon and baking powder. Add the flour to the mashed potatoes and work to a dough. Divide the dough and
roll out on a floured surface into 2 rounds, one
larger than the other. Place the larger one on a
greased baking tray. Peel, core and slice the
apples. Cover the pastry circle with the raw
apple slices. Dampen the edges and put the
other pastry round on top, pressing together to
seal the edges. Bake in a moderately hot oven
(190°) for 30-40 minutes or until golden brown.

Remove from the oven and carefully remove the upper crust. Sprinkle the apples with sugar and cinnamon and dot with butter. Replace the top and return to the oven for a few moments to allow the butter to melt. Serve whilst hot.

Apple and Elderberry Pie

Ingredients

350g (12 oz) flour, a pinch of salt, 350g (12
oz) butter, some milk, 4 large cooking apples
2 bunches of elderberries, 75g (3 oz) sugar,
castor sugar for dusting, 1 tablespoon honey

Method

Sieve the flour with the salt into a mixing bowl. Rub
the butter into the flour until it resembles fine
breadcrumbs. Add enough milk to form a stiff
dough. Leave the dough to stand at room temperature for about an hour. Roll out half the pastry onto
a floured surface. Cut out a circle large enough to
cover a 25cm (10 inch) plate. Grease the plate with
butter and line with the pastry. Peel, core and finely
slice the apples. Wash elderberries and destalk.
Sprinkle the elderberries over the apples and pour 1
tablespoon of water onto fruit, cover also with sugar
and honey. Roll out the remaining pastry and use to
cover the pie. Dampen the edges with water and
press well together. Sprinkle with caster sugar. Bake
in a moderately hot oven 200°C for about 45
minutes or until the pastry is golden brown.

꒜

Christmas Plum Pudding

Ingredients

225g (8 oz) flour, a pinch of salt, 1 teaspoon
baking powder, 2 teaspoons mixed spice,
225g (8 oz) fresh breadcrumbs, 225g (8 oz)
butter, 175g (6 oz) brown sugar, 375g (14 oz)
mixed dried fruit, 50g (2 oz) glacé cherries,
50g (2 oz) candied peel, 50g (2 oz) ground
almonds, 2 eggs beaten, 2 tablespoons honey
150ml whiskey, a drop of milk

Method

Sift together the flour, salt, baking powder and
spice. Add the breadcrumbs, butter and sugar,
mixing everything well together. Add the mixed
fruit, cherries, candied peel and almonds. Add
the beaten eggs, honey, whiskey and enough
milk to make a soft pudding mixture. Mix
everything thoroughly. Grease a pudding basin
and fill with the mixture allowing space at the
top of the basin for the pudding to rise. Cover
the basin with 2 sheets of grease proof paper,
securely tied. Steam in a pan of boiling water for

about 5 hours. Do not allow the pan to boil dry. Top up the water in the pan regularly. Serve flaming with more whiskey.

Home Made Custard Sauce

Ingredients

450ml (¾ pint) milk, 150ml (¼ pint) cream, 1 egg, 1 egg yolk, 1 teaspoon vanilla essence, 25g (1 oz) sugar or to taste

Method

Put a saucepan of cold water on the stove to boil. Beat the eggs, sugar and vanilla flavouring together until fluffy. Heat the milk and gradually stir it into the egg mixture. Put the custard into a bowl and stand it in the water to heat over a moderate heat. Stir with a wooden spoon until all the sugar is dissolved and the mixture coats the back of the spoon. Do not allow the custard to boil, or it will curdle. Pour into a warmed serving jug and serve hot. If serving cold, place grease proof paper, cut to size, over sauce to prevent a skin forming.

Hot Cross Buns

Ingredients

25g (1 oz) fresh yeast or 1½ teaspoons dried
yeast, 1 teaspoon castor sugar, 450g (1 lb)
flour, 1 teaspoon salt, 1 teaspoon mixed spice,
½ teaspoon cinnamon, ½ teaspoon nutmeg,
100g (4 oz) butter, 50g (2 oz) sugar,
50g (2 oz) currants, 50g (2 oz) raisins,
25g (1 oz) candied peel, 1 egg beaten,
300ml (½ pint) warm milk
For the glaze:
50g (2 oz) sugar, 4½ tablespoons milk

Method

Cream the yeast with a teaspoon of sugar. Mix
the flour, salt and spices in a bowl. Rub in the
butter. Add the sugar, fruit and candied peel.
Pour in the beaten egg, warmed milk and yeast.
Beat the ingredients together and work to a soft
dough. Knead the dough on a floured board for
5-10 minutes. Cover the dough with tinfoil and
leave in a warm place for about an hour until the
dough has doubled in size. Divide into 12 pieces

and shape into rounds. Place the rounds on a greased baking sheet. Cut crosses into each. Cover and leave to rise in a warm place for a further 30 minutes. Bake in a moderately hot oven (200°C) for about 20 minutes or until golden brown. Place in a cooling rack and glaze.

For the glaze:
Dissolve the sugar with the warmed milk. Brush the top of each bun with glaze whilst still warm. Serve immediately, buttered and with jam or honey.

Carragheen Pudding

Ingredients

15g (½ oz) Carragheen Moss, 900ml (1½
pints) milk, Grated rind of one lemon,
50g (2 oz) sugar

Method

Wash the Carragheen and leave it to soak in cold
water for 15 minutes. Drain well. Put the
Carragheen in a saucepan with the milk and the
lemon rind. Bring to the boil and simmer for
about 15 minutes. (For a less nutritious but
more *gentil* pudding attempt to strain out the
carragheen now). Add in the sugar and pour
into a moistened mould. Leave to set. Turn out
of the mould and decorate with whipped cream.

Bread and Butter Pudding

Ingredients

6 large slices of bread, 40g (1½ oz) butter or margarine, 50g (2 oz) sugar, 75g (3 oz) sultanas and raisins, 2 eggs, 1 tablespoon honey, 600ml (1 pint) milk, 25g sugar for the top, a pinch of nutmeg.

Method

Butter the bread on each side. If you prefer (and don't care about the world's starving millions) cut off the crusts. Cut the bread into large pieces. Cover the bottom of a greased 1ltr (2 pint) pie dish with a layer of bread, buttered side up. Sprinkle with sugar and dried fruit. Put another layer of bread, sugar and sultanas and final layer of bread on top, buttered side down. Beat the eggs with the milk and honey. Pour the egg mixture over the bread and leave to stand for at least ½ hour. Sprinkle the top with sugar and nutmeg and bake in a moderately hot oven (180°C) for about 1 hour.

Brown Bread Ice Cream

Ingredients

45g (1½ oz) wholemeal breadcrumbs, 500ml
whipping cream, 180g (6½ oz) demerara
sugar, 3 tablespoons of sweetish whiskey
(e.g. Bushmills Malt, Midleton Special),
a drop of vanilla essence

Method

Spread the crumbs out on a large tray and toast
under the grill, turning them regularly so they
brown on all sides. Remove from heat and leave
to cool. Stir crumbs into cream with the remaining ingredients. Cover and chill for one hour.

Restaurant

Recipes

Lettercollum House

Lettercollum House is a Victorian manor house, one mile from the village of Timoleague, Co. Cork. As well as being a renowned restaurant it provides reasonably-priced accommodation. Resident chef, Karen Austin, conducts courses in vegetarian cookery. Queries should be addressed to Lettercollum House, Timoleague, Co. Cork. Tel: 023-46251

Carrot and Orange Soup

Ingredients

7 carrots, 1 large onion, 1 large orange,
100g (4 oz) red lentils,
vegetable stock, salt and pepper

Method

Sauté onion and chopped carrots. Add vegetable stock, red lentils, grated zest of orange, salt and pepper. Bring to boil and simmer 40 minutes approx. Liquidise and add juice of orange. Adjust seasoning. Serve with a swirl of cream and chopped parsley.

Vegetable Mousakka

Ingredients

2 large aubergines
Tomato Sauce:
3 cloves garlic, 1 large onion, olive oil, 450g
(1 lb) tomatoes skinned and deseeded or large
tin tomatoes, 2 tablespoons tomato puree, ½
glass red wine, 100g (4 oz) cooked brown
lentils, salt and pepper, 2 tablespoons
chopped fresh basil or 1 teaspoon dried basil
Savoury Custard:
200ml (5 fl oz) cream, 3 egg yolks, 150g
(6 oz) cream cheese, 50g (2 oz) parmesan,
salt and black pepper

Method

Slice aubergines, sprinkle with salt, leave for 20
minutes approx. Rinse and pat dry. Smear the
aubergines with olive oil on both sides. Sauté the
onions until soft, add crushed garlic and cook
for a further 2 minutes. Stir in tomatoes, tomato
purée, red wine, lentils, salt and pepper. If using
dried basil add now. Simmer away for 10 min-

utes. If using fresh basil add now. Put cream, egg yolks and cream cheese in food processor and blend until smooth. Add parmesan cheese, salt and pepper. Put a third of the tomato mixture in the bottom of an oven proof dish, cover with half of the aubergines, then another third of the tomato mix with the remainder of the aubergines on top. Add the remainder of the tomato mix. Pour the savoury custard over the mixture and bake at 180°C for approx. 30 minutes until top is puffed and golden.

Summer Fruit Tart

Ingredients

1 sweet pastry base - baked blind.
Creme de patisserie:
3 egg yolks, 60g (2 oz) sugar, 20g (1 oz) flour,
250ml (½ pint) milk, ½ vanilla pod split,
Syrup: 100g (4 oz) sugar,
100ml (¼ pint) water
For glaze:
2 tablespoons apricot jam,
2 tablespoons water
Fresh fruit i.e. assortment of peaches,
plums and berry fruits

Method

Beat egg yolks with half of the sugar, sift in flour and mix well. Bring milk, the remaining sugar and vanilla pod to the boil. Pour, in a slow stream, beating all the time onto the egg yolk mixture. Return to saucepan and boil for 2 minutes. Cool and pour into pastry base. Dissolve sugar and water to make syrup. Add peaches and plums to syrup and poach for 10 minutes. (Do not poach berry fruits) Halve strawberries and arrange all of the fruit in a decorative pattern on top of the creme de patisserie. Bring apricot jam and water to the boil and strain. Brush over fruit and serve.

The Quay Co-op

The Quay Co-op restaurant is well established in all of the guide books. The building also includes a wholefood shop from which many of the more unusual ingredients found in this book can be bought. These recipes were devised by Dennis Cotter. All queries to The Quay Co-op, Sullivan's Quay, Cork City. Tel: 021-317660

Vegetable Tempura with Dipping Sauce

Ingredients

1 aubergine sliced into 1 cm thickness, 2 courgettes cut into 1 cm thickness, 4 carrots sliced quite thinly, 1 pepper (red or yellow) sliced, 1 cauliflower broken into florets, 1 broccoli stalk broken into florets, 4 whole radishes, 100g (4 oz) mange-tout, 100g (4 oz) mushrooms, 4 spring onions chopped into 5cm pieces
Batter:
100g (4 oz) sieved white flour, a pinch of salt 1 beaten egg yolk, 175ml (6 fl oz) water
Dip:
50g (2 oz) light tahini, 6 tablespoons hot water   3½ tablespoons soya sauce, ½ tablespoon honey, ½ tablespoon fine-grated ginger

Method

Make batter by combining all batter ingredients without overmixing and chill until needed. (Do not worry about lumps). Whisk tahini and hot water smooth, then beat in remaining ingredients. Heat oil to 180°C in deep-fat-fryer. Coat vegetables in batter, shake off excess and drop in oil, frying only one layer at a time. Keep cooked pieces warm while frying remainder. Serve on warmed plates with sauce in bowl, sprinkle with sesame seeds. Garnish with julienne ginger, slices of peppers, coconut strips and eat with chopsticks.

Aubergine and Tomato Red Wine Filo with Cucumber Raita and Goats Cheese and Walnut Salad

Aubergine and Tomato Red Wine Filo

Ingredients

300g (11 oz) aubergine, seed of 7 cardamom pods, ¼ teaspoon allspice (ground), ¼ teaspoon cayenne pepper, 1 whole bayleaf, ¾ teaspoon sugar, 110ml red wine, 110ml water, 2 teaspoon tomato puree, 90ml soya sauce, olive oil, 2 minced cloves of garlic, 100g (4 oz) fine breadcrumbs, 1 small, finely chopped onion, pinch salt, 50g (2 oz) finely chopped parsley, 225g (8 oz) fresh, chopped tomatoes, 16 sheets of filo pastry 22.5cm x 15cm (9" x 6").

Method

Sauté aubergines in olive oil until tender. Add cardamom seeds, allspice, cayenne pepper, bayleaf, sugar, red wine, water, tomato purée and soya sauce and simmer until reduced by a third. Do not let aubergines get mushy. Cool sauce and mix in the minced garlic cloves, breadcrumbs, finely chopped onion salt, chopped parsley and chopped tomatoes. Lightly butter 8 sheets of filo pastry on both sides. Place remaining 8 sheets on top and butter again. Put a large dessertspoon of filling at the top of each sheet, fold in 2.5cm on either side and roll up. Continue with remainder and place on a tray covered in grease proof paper and place in a pre-heated oven 240°C (460° F) for 15 to 20 minutes until golden brown.

꘡

Raita

Ingredients

½ cucumber, peeled and diced, 250ml
(½ pint) natural, unsweetened yoghurt, 1
minced clove of garlic, 1 teaspoon chopped
fresh mint, pinch of salt

Method

Combine all ingredients. Chill until needed.
Use within 24 hours.

Goats Cheese and Walnut Salad

Ingredients

Walnut vinaigrette:
1 teaspoon salt, 2 teaspoons red wine vinegar,
3 tablespoons olive oil, 4 tablespoons walnut
oil, freshly ground black pepper

❧

Salad:

1 head of oakleaf lettuce, 1 soft goats cheese,
4 tablespoons of chopped walnut

Method

Combine all vinaigrette ingredients and leave to stand until required. Wash lettuce, and divide between four serving bowls. Slice the goats cheese into four and lay on top of lettuce. Sprinkle each dish with a tablespoon of chopped walnuts. Finally drizzle vinaigrette over each salad. Serve the aubergine, red wine and tomato filos hot or cold with a ramekin of raita and a bowl of the walnut salad.

Cantaloupe and Ginger Sorbet with Blackberry Coulis

Ingredients

Sorbet:
1 ripe cantaloupe melon peeled, seeded and puréed, 225g (8 oz) granulated sugar, 110ml (3½ fl oz) water, 2 tablespoons lemon juice, 100ml (3¼ fl oz) ginger ale
Coulis:
250g (9 oz) fresh blackberries, 4 teaspoons water, 4 teaspoons caster sugar

Method

Heat sugar and water gently until sugar dissolves. Boil hard for about 20 minutes until syrupy (sugar thread stage). Add lemon juice and ginger ale and cool. Add melon pulp and pour into a polythene container and freeze overnight. Turn into a bowl and beat until smooth and creamy. Return to freezer until firm. Blend blackberries, sugar and water. Put the ingredients through a sieve. Slowly bring to the boil. Boil for 1 minute to a clear glossy sauce. Cool and chill. Serve by shaping sorbet with 2 large spoons. Place coulis on plates and place sorbet on top and garnish with fresh mint leaves.

Blazing Salads

Blazing Salads is located in the prestigious Powerscourt Townhouse Centre. All of their recipes are dairy, wheat and sugar free - so making them ideal for vegans, coeliacs and other people with special diets. These recipes were prepared by Lorraine Fitzmaurice. All queries to Blazing Salads, Powerscourt Townhouse Centre, Clarendon Street, Dublin 2. Tel: 01-6719552

Carrot and Cashew Nut Soup

Ingredients

1 medium onion diced finely, 75g (3 oz) cashew nut pieces, 675g (1½ lb) carrots cut into large rounds, 3 medium potatoes diced (optional), 900ml (1½ pints) water, sunflower oil, salt and pepper, chopped fresh parsley

Method

In a large saucepan sauté onion, cashew nuts in a little sunflower oil until golden brown. Add carrots, potatoes (if using) and sauté for a further 5 minutes. Season with salt and pepper. Add the water, cover and bring to boil. Simmer for 20 minutes. Liquidise well and season further. Garnish with chopped fresh parsley.

Steamed Vegetables in Sweet and Sour Sauce

Ingredients

1 carrot cut thickly, ¼ turnip diced, 1 small parsnip cut thickly, ½ cauliflower broken into florets, 1 small broccoli stalk broken into florets, 1 courgette cut thickly, 25g (1 oz) mange tout, 1 packet fresh baby sweet corn

Method

In a large saucepan put ½cm water and a pinch of salt. Add carrots and turnip, cover with a tight lid, bring to the boil, then reduce to the lowest heat possible and allow to steam. After approx. 5 minutes add parsnip, cauliflower, broccoli and cover for a further ten minutes. Add the courgette, mangetouts and corn, cover and steam until all the vegetables are tender.

Sweet and Sour Sauce

Ingredients

2 tsp arrowroot or cornflower, 30ml (1½ fl
oz) water, 30ml (1½ fl oz) soya sauce,
juice of half a lemon, 7 ml apple juice
concentrate, pinch of ginger, coriander
or parsley to garnish

Method

Blend all ingredients together. Heat until sauce
has thickened, stirring well to avoid lumps. Pour
over tossed, steamed vegetables.

Apple and Pear Crumble

Ingredients

2 dessert apples peeled and sliced, 2 dessert pears peeled and sliced, 25g (1 oz) raisins, 50g (2 oz) fine oatflakes, 50g (2 oz) jumbo oatflakes, 25g (1 oz) mix of pumpkin, sunflower and sesame seed, 3 tablespoons of apple concentrate, 3 tablespoons of sunflower oil

Method

Steam the apples and pears in a little water until tender, this takes approx. 5 minutes. Place fruit and liquid from same in oven proof dish together with 2 tablespoons of apple concentrate and raisins. In a bowl blend the oats and seeds with the sunflower oil and remaining apple concentrate. Spoon oat mixture over fruit and place in preheated oven (190°C) for 20-30 minutes until golden brown.

Cafe Paradiso

The Café Paradiso was opened up by Dennis Cotter (no relation to the editor) shortly before this book's first edition. Dennis was chef at the Quay Co-op for the previous five years. Since opening Dennis has won his way into the heart and stomach of many a food critic and guidebook compiler. Café Paradiso is situated opposite Jury's Hotel in Cork. All queries to Café Paradiso, 16 Lancaster Quay, Western Road, Cork City. Tel: 021-277939

※

Broccoli Mousse With Warm Tomato Vinaigrette

The Mousse ingredients

2 tablespoons olive oil or butter, 450g (10 oz) broccoli florets, 300ml light vegetable stock, 3 large eggs, 4-5 tablespoons cream, salt and pepper

Method

Preheat oven to 180°C. Half-fill a roasting tray with hot water and place on middle shelf. Sauté broccoli in oil for 3 minutes. Add stock, bring to boil, cover and simmer for 5 minutes. Cook 5 minutes more uncovered. Remove from heat, purée in a blender and season. Add eggs and cream and blend in. Butter six ramekins and fill each one with mixture. Place ramekins in the roasting tray and bake for 35 minutes. Allow to stand 5-10 minutes before turning out.

The Vinaigrette ingredients

3-4 tomatoes, skinned and chopped, 4-5
tablespoons red wine vinegar, 150ml olive oil,
30g shallots finely chopped (or a two-inch
piece of the white of a leek), small bunch
chives, finely chopped, salt and pepper

Method

Mix everything thoroughly and warm gently
in a pan.

Cheese Gougeres with Saffron-buttered Root Vegetables on Creamed Leeks

The Pastry

Ingredients

250ml hot water, 100g (4 oz) butter, 170g
(7 oz) flour, 100g (4 oz) cheese (Swiss-style or
cheddar), 3 medium-sized eggs,
pinch of cayenne, ½ tsp salt

Method

Preheat oven to (220°C). Place water and butter
in a saucepan and bring to boil. Add flour and
beat over low heat until smooth and shiny. Add
an egg and beat again until smooth. Repeat
process with remaining eggs before adding cheese
and seasoning. Now either pipe dough around

a large flan tin or pizza tray; or make 4 individual rings on a greased tray. Bake in oven for 10 minutes, then turn down heat to 100°C and bake for 5-10 minutes more.

The Vegetables

Ingredients

A selection of fresh root vegetables (e.g. Carrots, white turnip, swede, parsnip, celeriac)

Method

Dice the vegetables. Steam them until they are just tender. Season with salt and pepper.

The Butter

Ingredients

200g butter, a few sprigs of parsley, rind of ¼ lemon, pinch of cayenne pepper, ¼ tsp (or more!) saffron threads in 2 tablespoons of hot water.

Method

Blend everything

The Leeks

Ingredients

2 leeks, 2 cloves garlic, 50g (2 oz) butter,
250ml cream, pinch of nutmeg, salt and
pepper.

Method

Chop leeks and stew with garlic in the butter for
approx. 10 minutes. Add cream and seasoning.
Simmer until cream reduces by one third. Blend
half and replace in pot.

The Finale

If your timing is brilliant, place warm leeks on
a warm plate, place a straight-from-the-oven
gougère ring on top; then toss the hot vegetables
in the saffron butter and pour into the centres of
the gougères. If not, everything reheats well.
Serve with rice or potatoes for the root addicts.

Sauteed Pears with Ginger and Walnuts

Ingredients

4 pears peeled and cut in quarters or sixths, 50g (2 oz) walnut halves, 8 thin slices of fresh ginger, ½ glass of white wine, ½ glass of ginger syrup, home-made or deli-bought.

Method

Gently sauté pears in butter with walnuts for about six minutes, turning once. Add fresh ginger, cook for two minutes more. Add wine and syrup and allow to bubble once. Serve immediately with something, cold, creamy and rich — ice cream!

Mainistir House Hostel

Mainistir House Hostel located on the Aran Islands must be the last vegetarian eatinghouse before America. Cook Joel d'Anjou refuses to allow his establishment to be labelled a restaurant as most of the food is presented as a buffet, so it doesn't follow the usual divisions of starter, main-course and dessert. Whatever way it's presented its fame has spread far and wide. Below are some samples from Joel's buffet. All queries to Mainistir House Hostel, Inis Mór, Galway. Tel: 099 61169

Tomato Preserve

Ingredients

900g (2 lb) tomatoes, 900g (2 lb) sugar,
300ml (½ pint) water, 1 vanilla bean pod

Method

Place tomatoes in boiling water and leave to
stand for 5-10 minutes. Skin and cut into small
pieces, saving seeds and juices. Over a moderate
heat dissolve sugar and water. Add tomatoes and
leave to stand for 35 minutes. Add vanilla pod
and leave for another 10 minutes. Allow to cool
and serve with yoghurt, *fromage frais* or ricotta
cheese.

Caramelised Onions
And Prunes

Ingredients

3.6Kg (4 lb) onions, 900g (1 lb)
dried prunes, 900ml (1 pint) water,
225g (8 oz) butter, salt and pepper to taste

Method

Peel onions and cut into circles. Place in a heavy saucepan with water and prunes. Bring to a vigorous boil and let simmer until water has almost evaporated. Add butter and let it cook slowly until it is golden brown and all the ingredients are reduced to ¼ of its original contents. This may be served with nutty dishes or a sweet and sour accompaniment with tofu.

Cook up Rice

Ingredients

2 cups basmati rice, 1 dessert spoon butter, 1
cup of blackeyed beans, 1.2 ltr. (2 pints)
coconut milk, tabasco sauce or a few chopped
chillies, 2 onions, salt and pepper to taste

Method

Soak beans overnight, cook and leave to stand.
Coconut Milk:
Grate 1 coconut and add to water. Let stand.
Squeeze and discard shredded coconut. Fry
onions in butter until transparent. Add rice and
strained beans, then add milk and allow to cook
for 12 minutes until all the milk has been
absorbed. Add tabasco sauce and a knob of
butter and serve.

The Old Farmhouse

The Old Farmhouse is a secluded and peaceful guesthouse-restaurant at Greenane, Rathdrum, Co. Wicklow. Caroline Buck claims to have the largest herb garden in Co. Wicklow so you can count on her freshly-cooked meals being full of flavour. Caroline can be contacted at 0404-46676

Herb, Salad and Yoghurt Platter

Ingredients:

1 large tub plain yoghurt, 2 garlic cloves,
24 small nasturtium leaves, 24 sweet cicely
leaves, 24 small edible flowers, 12 radishes
sliced, a large bunch of parsley, a large bunch
of chives, 6 kiwi fruit, 6 sprigs of fennel,
1 cucumber

Method

I use these ingredients to decorate my starter
platter but really once you have prepared the
yoghurt which I choose to flavour with garlic
you could deviate and use whatever herbs or
salad you have to hand or prefer. Firstly grate the
garlic into the yoghurt using a grater — mix well
and then place a tablespoon in the centre of each
of the plates — spread this around the plate to
form a bed for the other ingredients (leave an

inch free around the outside of the plate) Now start to decorate the plates - from the outside place nasturtium leaves alternating with sweet cicely and place a small edible flower (e.g. daisy or rosemary) in the centre of each nasturtium leaf. Now coming onto the yoghurt bed decorate with a circle of cucumber, then a circle of parsley, then a circle of radish - finally peel the kiwi fruit and stand upright in the centre with a sprig of fennel in the top - sprinkle some chopped herbs over the kiwi fruit.

Tarragon and Turmeric Cheese Souffle

Ingredients:

150g (6 oz) butter, 100g (4 oz) self-raising
flour, milk, 6 lge free range eggs,
3 level teaspoons mustard (English), 2 level
teaspoons turmeric,
2 heaped teaspoons fresh chopped tarragon,
225g (8 oz) mature cheddar cheese (grated),
salt and pepper, sesame seeds

Method

I have found that this recipe gives a good, solid soufflé that doesn't FLOP. Preheat your oven to 250°C. Grease 2 soufflé dishes (8") using olive oil. Sprinkle sesame seeds around the soufflé dishes (just enough to stick to the oiled surfaces). Put milk, flour, cubed butter, mustard and turmeric into a saucepan on a low heat. Whisk continuously until mixture gets hot and starts to thicken. Remove from heat. Add cheese and seasoning and stir. Separate eggs, whisk whites until stiff in a basin large enough to hold all the mixture. Beat up yolks and add these to the sauce mixture. Stir well. Finally fold the sauce mixture into the whisked egg whites and stir well but lightly. Pour mixture into 2 dishes equally and place in the hot oven making sure that there is enough room for the soufflé to rise. Turn oven down to 180°C after 20 minutes and cook for a further 25 minutes. Don't be tempted to open the oven door during cooking. The soufflé is done when the top is risen, well browned and firm to the touch.

Blackcurrant Flan
with Meringue Topping

Ingredients

225g (8 oz) fineground wholemeal flour,
100g (4 oz) sunflower margarine, 2 eggs,
100g (4 oz) castor sugar, 450g (1 lb)
blackcurrants (any other fruit will do),
sugar to sweeten fruit

Method

Lightly stew fruit in as little water as possible
(very low heat will avoid burning) once fruit is
soft remove from heat and add sugar to taste.
Rub margarine and flour together in a mixing
bowl until mixture resembles breadcrumbs. Add
water a little at a time and mix until you can
press into a ball. Don't add too much water or
your pastry won't have that lovely crumbly
texture. If you have time pop your pastry into
the fridge (in a lunchbag or similar) for half an
hour as it will roll out better when cold. Start

rolling and don't worry if it breaks up, just piece it together like a jigsaw: it will taste just as good. Line a greased 10" flancase with the pastry and then spoon in the fruit. If the fruit has become very juicy save some of the juice for other things. Bake in a hot oven for 30 minutes and remove. Whisk the egg whites until they are stiff and fluffy and with the whisk running gradually add the castor sugar over about 4 minutes. Gently spread the meringue over the fruit and return to the hot oven for 5 minutes - then turn down the oven to 160°C and leave for a further 30 minutes. Serve hot with whipped fresh cream.

Phoenix Cafe

Shanahill, East Castlemaine, Co. Kerry. As well as a vegetarian Café the Phoenix is also a guesthouse offering hostel or private room accommodation. It is situated on the main Dingle-Killarney road three miles from Castlemaine and six miles from Inch strand. Lorna and Billy Tycher have a massive garden and as Lorna writes: 'Much of our stuff is created according to what the sun has ripened. I really have hundreds of spontaneous recipes in my head. Moving a glut of courgettes makes me work with other exciting sensations — colour, texture and those different areas of taste up and down the tongue!' the Tychers can be contacted on 066-66284

Mushroom & Sunflower Seed Pate

Ingredients

1 cup of sunflower seeds, 1 cup of chopped mushrooms, 1 cup of sunflower or vegan margarine, tamari, 3 garlic cloves, salt, pepper, lemon juice, pinch of cayenne pepper

Method

Dry roast sunflower seeds in a heavy-bottomed pan, sprinkle with sea salt. When seeds start turning slightly golden sprinkle generously with tamari, remove from heat and stir quickly. Leave to cool. Fry garlic and mushrooms until slightly golden. Add seasoning. Put everything in a food processor and grind to a paste. Test to see if seasoning is to your taste and adjust if necessary. Can be stored in an airtight container in a refrigerator for about four days. Serve in a paté dish on a plate decorated with salad leaves, olives (black), finely sliced cucumber and finely chopped tomatoes and toast.

Kofta Baked in Coconut Lemon and Ginger Sauce

Kofta Ingredients

225g (8 oz) breadcrumbs,
225g (8 oz) red split lentils,
225g (8 oz) sliced onion, 2 tbl of tomato
purée, cumin seeds, garlic clove sliced,
seasoning oil, garam masala and more bread
crumbs for dusting balls

Method

Boil lentils in just enough water to cook without making them too sloppy. If you find you have excess water just boil it off. Dry-roast cumin seeds in heavy-based pan over a high heat. Add oil, garlic, some garam masala and fry until garlic is golden brown. Lower heat to medium, add onions and breadcrumbs and keep turning for a few minutes. In a large mixing bowl combine everything and season to taste. The mixture should be firm but not dry. Divide the mixture into golfball sizes and coat with a combination of breadcrumbs, a pinch of garam masala and salt. Lightly oil a baking tray and bake in a moderate oven (180°C) for 45 minutes until baked golden brown. Remove from oven and leave to cool under a teatowel. When lifting from tray be careful not to cause them to crumble. Koftas can be stored in a fridge for three days or frozen.

Sauce ingredients

10 whole cardamom pods, thumb sized knob of fresh ginger, 4 garlic cloves,
2 lemons, 100 gm (2oz) of pure creamed coconut (½ pack), 2 tbl of flour, tandoori curry paste, mustard paste

Method

Break-up cordamom pods and lightly dry-roast the seeds in a frying-pan or griddle over a medium heat, add oil, garlic and curry paste. When oil is sizzling add flour and fry until it bubbles and starts to brown — remove from heat. Add water, chopped ginger, lemon zest and juice, coconut and mustard. Bring to the boil, stirring until thick, then reduce heat and let simmer for at least five minutes.

Crunchy topping ingredients

Equal quantities of oat flakes, bread crumbs,
raisins and bombay mix.
Put everything in a coffee or spice grinder
until ground. Should be slightly course.

Preparation of a single portion:

Place two kofta balls in an oiled oven-proof dish.
Bake in a hot oven for 10 minutes. Meanwhile
heat 2 soup ladles of sauce. Remove balls from
oven and pour sauce over. Cover with a generous
sprinkling of the crunchy topping and a finely
chopped tomato. Cover all with a sheet of foil
and bake until sauce starts to sizzle. Remove foil
for 30 seconds so crunchy topping can brown.
But beware as topping can burn quite easily.
Serve with chopped fresh coriander or parsley
and a portion of brown rice or cous cous or
bulgur wheat.

Chilled Apricot Crumble

Ingredients

About four coffee mugs of dried apricots
(preferably sulphur free), vanilla, cinnamon
sticks, a glass of orange juice and a
glass of red wine, 100g (4 oz) of white flour,
100g (4 oz) of digestive biscuit
or whole grain flour, 100g (4 oz) of sunflower
margarine, 100g (4 oz) of brown sugar
(only half that if biscuits used)
50g (2 oz) of chopped, mixed nuts

Method

Soak apricots in water overnight. Drain and
cook in orange juice and wine with vanilla and
cinnamon until the liquid forms a heavy syrup.
Remove cinnamon sticks. Place in an ovenproof
dish. Rub crumble ingredients together and
press onto apricots. Cover and bake quite hot
(220°C) for 30 minutes. Remove cover and
bake for a further 15 minutes. Remove from
oven, leave to cool, then chill. Serve upside
down slices or wedges, decorated with crunchy

almonds. See below.

Toast almonds in sunflower margarine and some sugar in a heavy based pan. Stir until sugar melts. Remove from heat and allow to cool, stirring occasionally to keep mixture broken-up.

An Taelann, Killarney

7 Bridewell Lane, New Street, Killarney, Co. Kerry. Deirde Donohue offers delicious, nutritious food using organic produce when possible. She also bakes her own bread, desserts and cakes. If you're in Killarney you must go there! Contact Deirdre on 064-33083

Courgette Fritters
with Tzatziki

Fritter ingredients

450g (1lb) courgettes grated, 75g (3 oz)
farmhouse cheddar or mozzarella cheese
grated, 1 free range egg slightly beaten, 1 tbl
of freshly-chopped parsley, 1 tsp dried dill
weed, 25g (1 oz) plain flour, 25g (1 oz) corn-
meal, salt and freshly-ground pepper,
vegetable oil for frying

Method

Mix together grated courgette, cheese, and egg.
Add herbs and seasoning. Add flour and corn-
meal. Heat oil in pan. Shallow fry heaped tablespoons of the mixture until fairly firm and
golden on both sides. Drain on kitchen paper
and serve hot with the tsatziki.

Tsatziki ingredients

1 cucumber (preferably organic) peeled and finely chopped or grated, 1 tbl of chopped fresh mint. 1-2 cloves garlic crushed, 150 ml (¼ pint) of plain natural yoghurt or Greek yoghurt, salt and freshly ground pepper

Method

Mix all the ingredients in a bowl and stir well. Set aside for at least half an hour for the flavours to infuse.

Tofu and Ginger Stir-fry

Ingredients

225g (8 oz) firm tofu in ½cm cubes, 2 tsp
grated fresh root ginger, ½ cup tamari/soya
sauce, ½ cup of water, 2 garlic cloves finely
chopped, 2 onions chopped,
2 carrots cut in fine julienne strips,
100g (4 oz) mangetouts cut diagonally,
1 cup mixed seasonal vegetables (mushrooms, courgettes, broccoli, peppers etc.),
50g (2 oz) hazlenuts (toasted),
350g (12 oz) cooked short-grain brown rice,
parsley or cress to garnish

Method

In a shallow dish, marinade the tofu in the
tamari and water adding garlic and ginger. Leave
for at least an hour for the flavours to infuse. In
a wok gently sauté onion in butter or olive oil for
a few minutes. Add the rest of the vegetables and
sauté for 5-10 minutes, making sure they don't
burn. Add the tofu with marinade, the cooked

rice and hazelnuts. Cover and simmer gently, stirring occasionally, for 5-10 minutes or until vegetables are tender. Season with pepper and garnish with fresh parsley or cress.

Date and Walnut Flan

Ingredients

225g (8 oz) shortcut pastry, 225g (8 oz) raw cane sugar, 130g (5 oz) chopped walnuts, 225g (8 oz) chopped dates, 300ml (½ pint) of cream

Method

Roll out chilled pastry to fit a 9" flan dish. Preheat oven to 200°C and when hot bake for 15 minutes until pastry is set. Place the sugar in a saucepan with a drop of water and melt over a low heat until it carmelises. Remove from heat, stir in the walnuts, dates and cream. Return to the heat and boil for 3-4 minutes, stirring all the time to prevent the mixture from burning. Pour mixture into the flan case and allow to set — then refrigerate. Serves 8-10

Drimcong House

Drimcong House is a beautiful lakeside 300 year old estate house in Moycullen Co. Galway, 15 minutes west of Galway city. Resident chef Gerry Galvin was Egon Ronay chef of the year for 1994. Gerry runs vegetarian courses from time to time and can be contacted at 091-85115/85585. Open March-December.

Tomato, Onion and Pesto Salad in Balsamic Dressing

Ingredients

10 medium ripe tomatoes sliced, 2 medium onions finely chopped, 200ml ($^1/_3$ pint) balsamic vinegar, 3 tablespoons olive oil, 1 tablespoon pesto, seasoning

Method

Put sliced tomatoes in a bowl and sprinkle chopped onion on top. Spoon pesto over onion. Mix and season the dressing ingredients i.e. oil and vinegar and pour over salad. Before serving test for seasoning again and mix everything gently. Serve on a bed of lettuce leaves.

Baked Avocado with Pickled Carrots and Toasted Nuts

Ingredients

3 ripe avocados, 6 medium carrots grated, 2
tablespoon chopped dill or lemon balm, 1.5
pints good white wine vinegar, 150g (6 oz)
castor sugar, 1 level teaspoon ground ginger,
2 tablespoon white wine, juice of two oranges
2 oz chopped mixed nuts, toasted,
salt and pepper

Method

Prepare pickling liquid by heating together vinegar, sugar, wine, juice and ginger. Bring to the boil and stir until sugar dissolves. Add dill or lemon balm and pour over grated carrot. Pack into warm sterilised jars and seal. Peel and halve avocados and cut a thin slice from the bottom of each half so that they sit evenly. Put Avocado halves in a baking dish, spoon carrot pickle into their cavities and pour liquid over the base of the dish. Season, cover with foil and bring to the boil on top of the stove. Transfer to oven and bake for 10 minutes. Sprinkle nuts over avocados and serve.

NB for large appetites you may want to use 6 avocados for this recipe!

Hot Chocolate Pudding in Sabayon Sauce

Oven: 220°C

Ingredients:

130g (5 oz) good, plain chocolate, 2 tablespoons butter, 3 Eggs, 3 tablespoons castor
sugar

Method:

Melt chocolate and one tablespoon butter over
low heat in a heavy-based saucepan. Remove
from heat and pour into a deep bowl. Separate
eggs. Whisk whites to stiff peaks with castor
sugar. Beat yolks into the butter and chocolate.
Stir ¼ of the meringue mixture into the chocolate and fold in the rest. At this stage the mixture
can be refrigerated for a couple of hours before
baking or the process can be completed as
follows:

Butter 3¼ inch diameter ramekins with the remaining tablespoon butter and fill ³/₄ inch full with chocolate mixture. Bake for about 20 minutes until well risen. Remove from oven and rest in a warm place while you make the sauce.

Sabayon Sauce ingredients:

4 egg yolks, 90g (3½) oz castor sugar, 200ml white wine, a tablespoon lemon juice

Method:

Put all the ingredients in a bowl over a pot of simmering water. The water should not touch the base of the bowl. Whisk until the sabayon is thick and starting to come away from the sides of the bowl about — 10 minutes in all.

Bavaria House

Rolf and Ilse Kiebler are the hosts at this wonderful guest house at Garrymore, Ballinagh, Co. Cavan. Ilse loves to prepare meals from her own organically grown vegetables and fruit. As well as feeding you well the Kieblers can arrange watersports and other outdoor pursuits during your stay. All queries to Ilse on 049-37452. English and German spoken.

Jerusalem Artichoke Salad

Ingredients

600g Jerusalem artichoke, 3 tbs lemon Juice,
3 tbs sunflower oil, 2 tbs roasted sesame seed,
a handful of portulak leaves
or parsley, a pinch of seasalt

Method

Scrub, wash and grate the artichokes, add lemon
juice, oil, sesame seed and salt, stir well, sprinkle
the washed portulak leaves over each portion.

Potatoes with Leek, Tofu and Mustard Sauce

Ingredients

1 kg small unpeeled potatoes, 1 kg leeks, 800g tofu, seasalt and soya sauce

Mustard Sauce ingredients

50ml soy oil, 60g wholemeal, 2 tbs mustard, 400ml water, 200ml milk (soymilk), seasalt, pepper, lemon juice

Heat the oil, add the wholemeal and the mustard, pour in the water and milk, stir well, reduce the heat, add salt, pepper, lemon juice to taste and simmer for about 20 minutes. Steam the washed potatoes for about 25 minutes. Wash the leek, cut it in 1 cm rings and steam for not longer than 6 minutes (after the water is boiling). Sprinkle the tofu on both sides with seasalt and soya sauce (few drops), heat the pan with a tablespoon of sunflower oil and fry the tofu for 3 minutes each side.

Fresh Fruit Salad

Ingredients for dessert:

3 oranges, 3 bananas, 3 kiwis, 1 lemon, 1 lime, 200ml gin or vodka, whipped cream and chocolate flakes for decoration

Method

Cut the oranges, bananas and kiwis into bitesize pieces, put them into a bowl, add the juice of the lemon and lime and gin, stir well, garnish with whipped cream and sprinkle the chocolate flakes (carobs) on top.

Natural Foods

Wendy O'Byrne's Natural Foods has been established in Paul Street Cork for almost two decades. As well as providing the denizens of Cork and further afield with essential ingredients for their wholefood cooking, Natural Foods sells fresh wholemeal breads and cakes baked on the premises. Regular patrons are often lucky enough to leave Wendy's with her wholemeal loaves, buns or pizzas still steaming hot in their hands.

Overleaf is a recipe for one of Wendy's most popular, original, sweetthings.

Wendy's Apricot and Almond Slices

This tasty tray-bake can be eaten hot or cold — as a dessert or as a cold slice. It is especially suitable for people trying to stay off the sugar or for those on a wheat-free diet.

Ingredients

Topping and base: 550g (1 lb 4 oz) oatflakes, 225g (8 oz) fine oatmeal, 125g (5 oz) almonds (flaked in blender) ½ tsp ground ginger, 225g (8 oz) vegetable margarine, 1 heaped tablespoons malt extract, 80 ml apple concentrate and 20 ml (approx) water. Filling: 450g (1lb) dried apricots, 6 drops of almond essence.

Method

Wash dried apricots and barely covering them with water, stew gently until soft. When cooled, mash together with almond essence. Combine oatflakes, oatmeal, almonds and ginger in a large bowl. Warm margarine and malt extract together in a pan and then rub into the oat mixture, Gradually trickle in the apple concentrate and finally the water and mix lightly with fingertips. Grease a flapjack tray and spread ½ the oat-mixture, firming down well. Then spread the apricots and lastly sprinkle the rest of the oat-mixture over the apricots until fully covered. Press lightly with a rolling-pin. Bake in a medium oven (180° C) for about 50 minutes.

The Doolin Cafe

The Doolin Café is situated in Doolin Co. Clare. It is run by John and Josephine Clinton. John writes:

"A description of the Doolin Café is hard but perhaps the best is what our customers have to say. The Doolin Café is different. 'An oasis for vegetarians travelling in Ireland,' said one customer. Pictures on the walls, books on the shelves and music to please.

'I felt I like I was at home, good food….cheerful atmosphere…great music,' said another. Warmth and positive karma fill the Doolin Café."

John and Josephine can be reached by phone or fax on 065-74429

Crunchy Salad

Ingredients

6 stalks celery chopped, 3 red dessert apples for colour unpeeled and chopped, sultanas to taste, olive oil, juice of half a lemon, 1 green pepper chopped, roasted sunflower seeds, chopped nuts

Method

Chop and mix celery, green pepper, sultanas, sunflower seeds and nuts. Mix oil and lemon juice together and add apple-pieces, mixing thoroughly. Add this to the celery and green pepper and mix together. Taste for crunch and nuttiness. The lemon juice will stop the apples going brown. If preparing some time before serving leave the apples unchopped and mix at the last minute. You can roast the sunflower seeds and nuts together to give a good flavour. Put these into a frying pan with a little olive oil and salt. Heat the pan and stir until the seeds and nuts are golden brown. Do not leave in pan otherwise they will burn.

Bean Stew with Stir-fry Vegetables

Ingredients

170g (6 oz) blackeyed beans (soaked overnight), 170g (6 oz) haricot beans
(soaked overnight), 2 onions chopped, 1
onion halved, 2 green peppers de-seeded
and chopped, 2 red peppers de-seeded and
chopped, 2 cloves garlic crushed, 2 tins 400g
(14 oz) chopped tomatoes, 2 tbs concentrated
tomato purée, 2 tbs olive oil, ground cumin,
bouquet garni, ground black pepper and salt
to taste

Method

For the vegetable stir fry select any combination
of fresh seasonal vegetables, washed, drained
and cut up into bite size chunks. 60g (2 oz)
roasted sunflower seeds. 1 tbs sesame oil (for
good taste) or olive oil. Drain the beans and
place in a saucepan of fresh cold water. Add the
onion halves, bouquet garni and pinch of ground

cumin. Boil for 10 minutes stirring well and reduce heat. Simmer for about 40 minutes or until the beans are almost tender. Strain, reserving half of the stock. Discard onion and bouquet garni. Heat the oil in a large saucepan. Sweat the onions for 5 minutes. Add garlic, peppers, good pinch ground cumin. Mix well and continue to sweat for 10 minutes. Using a wok or heavy frying pan, stir fry the vegetables and sunflower seeds in oil for 1 to 3 minutes stirring all the time. Spoon the vegetables and sunflower seeds over the bean stew and serve immediately with hot boiled new potatoes.

Cinnamon Oranges

Ingredients

6 sweet oranges, 2 to 3 tbs sugar, water, juice of one small lemon, 1 tsp powdered cinnamon, 1 stick cinnamon

Method

Peel the oranges closely with a sharp knife removing all the pith. Cut into thin rounds and lay them on a large plate. Sprinkle each layer with powdered cinnamon. Heat 140 ml ($^1/_4$ pint) water with the sugar. Simmer, stirring frequently for 5 minutes until syrup forms. Add the lemon juice and pour over the oranges. Break the cinnamon stick into splinters and place on top of the oranges. Chill well. Remove cinnamon splinters before serving.

Oven Temperatures

Degrees Centigrade	Degrees Fahrenheit	Regulo (for gas cookers)
115-35	240-80	¼-½
135-60	280-320	1
160-70	320-40	3
170-85	340-70	4
185-205	370-400	5-6
205-25	400-40	7
225-50	440-80	8-9